MASTERING YOUR EARNINGS

Unlocking The Secrets To Financial Freedom

Frank A. Hyman

Table of Contents:

Introduction

Welcome to a transformative journey towards financial empowerment and prosperity! In this comprehensive guide, 'Mastering Your Earnings,' we delve deep into the art of managing your income, uncovering practical strategies and timeless wisdom to help you take control of your financial destiny.

In an ever-changing economic landscape, it has become increasingly crucial to navigate the complexities of money management with skill and precision. Whether you're a seasoned investor, a recent graduate, or someone looking to break free from the shackles of financial insecurity, this book is designed to cater to all levels of financial literacy.

Through thought-provoking insights and step-by-step guidance, you'll learn how to optimize your earnings, create multiple streams of income, and make informed decisions that align with your long-term goals. We explore the principles of budgeting, saving, investing, and avoiding common financial pitfalls, empowering you to make smarter choices with your hard-earned money.

Dive into the psychology of money, understand your personal financial mindset, and uncover the barriers that may be holding you back from reaching your fullest earning potential. Discover how to cultivate a mindset of abundance, leveraging your unique skills and passions to maximize your earning capacity.

'Mastering Your Earnings' isn't just about amassing wealth, but about creating a life of financial independence, security, and fulfillment. With the right knowledge and dedication, you can pave the way for a brighter future, where you are in control of your financial destiny.

Are you ready to embark on this transformative journey? Let the pages ahead be your guide to unlocking the path of financial freedom and mastering your earnings."

Chapter 1:

Understanding the Importance of Earnings

Earnings are a company's profits, and they are one of the most important financial metrics that investors and analysts use to assess a company's performance. Earnings are important for a number of reasons:

They provide a measure of a company's profitability. Earnings are a measure of how much money a company is making after all of its expenses have been paid. This is a key metric for investors because it shows how well a company is managing its resources and generating profits.

They help to determine a company's valuation. The price-to-earnings (P/E) ratio is a common valuation metric that is used to compare the price of a company's stock to its earnings. A higher P/E ratio means that investors are willing to pay more for a company's stock based on its earnings.

They can signal future performance. Earnings can provide investors with insights into how a company is likely to perform in the future. For example, if a company is consistently reporting strong earnings, it is likely that the company will continue to perform well in the future.

They can impact a company's stock price. When a company reports earnings that are better than expected, the stock price of the company will typically go up. Conversely, if a company reports earnings that are worse than expected, the stock price of the company will typically go down.

In short, earnings are an important financial metric that can provide investors with valuable insights into a company's performance.

Earnings can help investors to determine whether a company is a good investment, and they can also impact the price of a company's stock.

Additional points about the importance of earnings:

Earnings are not the only factor that matters to investors. Other factors, such as a company's growth prospects, its competitive landscape, and its management team, can also be important to investors. However, earnings are a key factor that investors consider when making investment decisions.

Earnings can be manipulated. In some cases, companies may engage in earnings management in order to make their earnings look better than they actually are. This can make it difficult for investors to assess a company's true profitability.

Earnings should be considered in the context of other financial metrics. Earnings should not be viewed in isolation. Investors should consider earnings in the context of other financial metrics, such as revenue, cash flow, and debt levels. This will help investors to get a more complete picture of a company's financial health.

Overall, earnings are an important financial metric that can provide investors with valuable insights into a company's performance. However, it is important to remember that earnings are not the only factor that matters to investors, and they should be considered in the context of other financial metrics.

Setting Financial Goals

What are financial goals? Financial goals are specific, measurable, achievable, relevant, and time-bound objectives that you set for yourself to improve your financial situation. They can be short-term, medium-term, or long-term, and they can be anything from saving for a down payment on a house to paying off debt to retiring comfortably.

Why are financial goals important?

Setting financial goals is important for a number of reasons. First, it gives you a sense of direction and purpose. When you know what you're working towards, it's easier to stay motivated and on track. Second, financial goals can help you build wealth. By setting specific goals and making a plan to achieve them, you can start to grow your financial assets over time. Third, financial goals can help you reduce stress. When you have a plan for your money, you're less likely to worry about unexpected expenses or financial setbacks.

How to set financial goals

There are a few steps involved in setting financial goals:

Figure out what you want to achieve. What are your financial priorities? What do you want to achieve with your money? Once you know what you want, you can start to set specific goals.

Make your goals SMART. Your goals should be specific, measurable, achievable, relevant, and time-bound. This will help you stay focused and on track.

Create a plan. Once you know what your goals are, you need to create a plan to achieve them.

This may involve setting a budget, creating a savings plan, or investing your money.

Track your progress. It's important to track your progress towards your goals so that you can see how you're doing and make adjustments as needed.

Types of financial goals

There are four main types of financial goals:

Short-term goals are those that you can achieve within a year or two. Examples of short-term financial goals include saving for a down payment on a house, paying off debt, or taking a vacation.

Medium-term goals are those that you can achieve within five to ten years. Examples of medium-term financial goals include saving for a child's education, saving for retirement, or starting a business.

Long-term goals are those that you can achieve within 10 to 30 years or more. Examples of long-term financial goals include saving for retirement, leaving a legacy, or achieving financial independence.

Setting financial goals is an important step in taking control of your finances and achieving your financial dreams. By following the steps above, you can set SMART goals, create a plan, and track your progress towards your financial goals.

Tips for setting financial goals:

Be realistic about your goals. Don't set yourself up for failure by setting unrealistic goals.

Be flexible. Your goals may change over time, so be prepared to adjust them as needed.

Setting financial goals is a journey, not a destination. By setting SMART goals, creating a plan, and tracking your progress, you can achieve your financial dreams.

Chapter 2:

The Psychology of Earnings

The psychology of earnings is a complex topic that encompasses a variety of factors, including individual expectations, market sentiment, and economic conditions. However, some general trends can be observed.

Confirmation bias: People tend to interpret new information in a way that confirms their existing beliefs. This can lead to investors being more likely to buy stocks that have recently performed well, and to sell stocks that have recently performed poorly.

Anchoring bias: People tend to place too much weight on the first piece of information they receive. This can lead to investors being influenced by the earnings reports of other companies in the same industry, even if those companies are not directly comparable.

Loss aversion: People tend to be more motivated by the avoidance of losses than by the pursuit of gains. This can lead to investors being more likely to sell stocks after they have experienced a decline in price, even if the long-term outlook for the company is positive.

In addition to these general trends, the psychology of earnings can also be influenced by specific events, such as changes in interest rates or political uncertainty. As a result, it is important for investors to be aware of the psychological factors that can affect their investment decisions.

Here are some additional examples of how the psychology of earnings can impact investors:

Earnings surprises: When a company's earnings report is better or worse than expected, it can have a significant impact on the stock price. This is because investors are often surprised by earnings reports, and they may overreact to the news.

Earnings momentum: If a company has a history of strong earnings growth, investors may be more likely to buy its stock, even if the current earnings report is not as strong as expected. This is because investors may believe that the company is likely to continue to grow its earnings in the future.

Earnings guidance: When a company provides guidance for future earnings, it can also impact the stock price. This is because investors use guidance to assess the company's outlook, and they may adjust their investment decisions accordingly.

The psychology of earnings is a complex and ever-changing topic. However, by understanding the factors that can influence investor behavior, investors can make more informed investment decisions.

Overcoming Limiting Beliefs About Money

Here are some tips on how to overcome limiting beliefs about money:

Identify your limiting beliefs. The first step is to identify the limiting beliefs that you have about money. What are the thoughts and beliefs that hold you back from achieving your financial goals? Once you know what your limiting beliefs are, you can start to challenge them.
Challenge your beliefs. Once you have identified your limiting beliefs, it's time to challenge

them. Ask yourself if these beliefs are really true. Are they based on facts or on assumptions? Are they based on your past experiences or on your current reality? Once you start to challenge your beliefs, you may find that they are not as true as you thought they were.

Reframe your beliefs. Once you have challenged your limiting beliefs, you can start to reframe them. This means changing the way you think about money. For example, if you believe that "money is the root of all evil," you could refrain that belief to "money is a tool that can be used for good or evil."

Practice positive affirmations. Positive affirmations can be a powerful tool for changing your mindset about money. When you repeat positive affirmations to yourself, you are essentially programming your subconscious mind with new beliefs. Some examples of positive affirmations about money include:

"I am worthy of having financial abundance."

"I am good with money."

"I am able to create wealth."

Take action. The final step is to take action. This means making changes to your financial habits and behaviors. If you want to change your beliefs about money, you need to start acting in a way that is consistent with those new beliefs. For example, if you want to believe that "money is a tool that can be used for good," you could start by donating money to charity or investing in a social enterprise.

Overcoming limiting beliefs about money takes time and effort, but it is possible. By following these tips, you can start to change your mindset about money and achieve your financial goals.

Here are some guidelines that can help you overcome limiting beliefs about money:

Find a financial mentor or coach. A financial mentor or coach can help you identify your limiting beliefs and develop a plan to overcome them.

Join a financial support group. A financial support group can provide you with the support and encouragement you need to change your mindset about money.

Read books and articles about financial success. Reading about the experiences of others who have overcome limiting beliefs about money can help you believe that it is possible for you to do the same.

Visualize your financial goals. Take some time each day to visualize yourself achieving your financial goals. This will help you stay motivated and focused on your journey.

Remember, changing your mindset about money is a process. There will be setbacks along the way, but don't give up. Keep challenging your beliefs, practicing positive affirmations, and taking action. With time and effort, you will eventually overcome your limiting beliefs and achieve your financial goals.

Developing a Positive Money Mindset

Your money mindset is the underlying belief system you have about money. It's the way you think about money, how you feel about it, and how you use it. Your money mindset can have a big impact on your financial well-being.

A positive money mindset is one that is based on abundance, opportunity, and self-worth. People with a positive money mindset believe that they have the power to control their financial future and that they deserve to be financially successful. They are also more likely to be financially literate and to have good financial habits.

If you want to develop a positive money mindset, there are a few things you can do:

Forgive your past financial mistakes. Everyone makes financial mistakes at some point in their lives. The important thing is to learn from them and move on. Don't let your past mistakes hold you back from achieving your financial goals.

Understand your thoughts and emotions surrounding money. What are your beliefs about money? Do you think of it as a scarce resource or an abundant one? Do you feel guilty about spending money or do you enjoy it? Once you understand your thoughts and emotions about money, you can start to change them.

Realize that comparing yourself to others is a losing game. Everyone's financial situation is different. Comparing yourself to others will only make you feel bad about yourself. Instead, focus on your own goals and progress.

Work on forming good habits. This includes budgeting, saving, and investing. It's also important to be mindful of your spending habits. Once you develop good habits, they will become second nature and you'll be more likely to stick to them.

Create a budget that brings you joy. A budget doesn't have to be restrictive. It can be a tool that helps you make the most of your money and reach your financial goals. When you create a budget, make sure to include some money for things that you enjoy.

Remember to be thankful. When you're grateful for what you have, it's easier to have a positive attitude about money. Take some time each day to reflect on the things you're grateful for, both big and small.

Developing a positive money mindset takes time and effort, but it's worth it. When you have a positive attitude about money, you're more likely to make good financial decisions and achieve your financial goals.

Additional tips that may help you develop a positive money mindset:

Read books and articles about financial literacy and personal finance. This will help you learn more about money and how to manage it effectively.

Talk to a financial advisor. A financial advisor can help you create a budget, develop a financial plan, and reach your financial goals.

Join a financial support group. This can be a great way to connect with others who are on the same journey as you and learn from their experiences.

Celebrate your successes. When you reach a financial goal, take some time to celebrate your success. This will help you stay motivated and on track.

Developing a positive money mindset is an ongoing process. There will be setbacks along the way, but don't give up. Just keep learning, growing, and making progress. With time and effort, you can develop a positive money mindset that will help you achieve your financial goals.

Chapter 3:

Maximizing Your Income Potential

Tips on how to maximize your income potential:

Set clear financial goals. What do you want to achieve with your money? Do you want to buy a house, save for retirement, or start your own business? Once you know what you want, you can start making a plan to reach your goals.

Increase your skills and education. The more skills you have, the more valuable you will be to employers. Consider taking some courses, getting a certification, or even going back to school.

Network with people in your field. The people you know can be a great source of new opportunities. Attend industry events, join professional organizations, and reach out to people on LinkedIn.

Be willing to relocate. If you're serious about increasing your income, you may need to be willing to move to a different city or state. There are often more opportunities in larger cities, and the cost of living may be lower in other areas.

Start a side hustle. A side hustle can be a great way to generate extra income and learn new skills. There are many different side hustles you can do, such as freelancing, starting a blog, or selling products online.

Invest your money. When you invest your money, you're essentially putting it to work for you. Over time, your investments can grow and provide you with a steady stream of income.

Be patient and persistent. It takes time and effort to increase your income potential. Don't get discouraged if you don't see results immediately. Just keep working hard and eventually you will reach your goals.

Here are some additional tips:

Get organized. Keep track of your expenses and income so you can see where your money is going. This will help you make informed decisions about how to spend and save your money.

Live below your means. This means spending less money than you earn. By living below your means, you'll have more money to save and invest.

Manage your debt. If you have debt, focus on paying it off as quickly as possible. This will free up more money in your budget so you can save and invest.

Protect your assets. Get life insurance, disability insurance, and other types of insurance to protect your financial future.

By following these tips, you can increase your income potential and achieve your financial goals.

Navigating Career Advancement

Navigating career advancement can be a daunting task, but it is definitely possible with careful planning and execution. Here are some key tips to help you on your journey:

Set clear goals. What do you want to achieve in your career? Once you know what you want, you can start to develop a plan to get there. Your goals should be specific, measurable, achievable, relevant, and time-bound.

Identify your strengths and weaknesses. What are you good at? What do you need to improve on? Once you know your strengths and weaknesses, you can start to focus on developing the skills you need to achieve your goals.

Get involved in professional development. This could involve taking courses, attending conferences, or networking with other professionals in your field. Professional development is a great way to learn new skills, stay up-to-date on industry trends, and build your network.

Be a top performer. This means consistently meeting or exceeding expectations, going above and beyond your job description, and being a team player. If you are a top performer, you will be more likely to be noticed by your manager and considered for promotions.

Be proactive. Don't wait for opportunities to come to you. Instead, be proactive and seek out opportunities to take on new challenges and responsibilities. This will show your manager that you are ambitious and eager to advance your career.

Build relationships. Networking is an important part of career advancement. Get to know people in your field and build relationships with them. This will help you stay up-to-date on industry trends, learn about new opportunities, and get your foot in the door.

Be patient. Career advancement takes time and effort. Don't get discouraged if you don't see results immediately. Just keep working hard and stay focused on your goals.

Following these tips will help you navigate career advancement and achieve your goals. Just remember to be patient, persistent, and willing to work hard. With time and effort, you will reach your full potential.

Here are some additional tips:

Be a good communicator. This includes being able to write and speak clearly and concisely.
Be a team player. Be willing to help out your colleagues and be supportive of their success.
Be positive and enthusiastic. This will make you more approachable and likable, which will help you build relationships with others.
Be open to feedback. Be willing to listen to feedback from your manager and colleagues, and use it to improve your performance.
Navigating career advancement can be a challenge, but it is definitely possible with hard work and dedication. By following these tips, you can increase your chances of success.

Negotiating Salaries and Benefits

Negotiating salaries and benefits can be a daunting task, but it's important to do your research and be prepared if you want to get the best possible offer. Here are some tips to help you negotiate your salary and benefits:

Do your research. Before you start negotiating, you need to know what the market rate is for your position and experience level. You can use online salary calculators, industry surveys, or talk to your network to get this information.

Be prepared to walk away. If you're not happy with the offer, be prepared to walk away from the negotiation. This will show the employer that you're serious about getting what you want.

Be confident. When you're negotiating, it's important to be confident in your abilities. This will help you get the best possible offer.

Be prepared to compromise. It's unlikely that you'll get everything you want in a negotiation. Be prepared to compromise on some things in order to get what's most important to you.

Be professional. Even though you're negotiating, it's important to be professional at all times. This means being respectful of the other party and keeping your emotions in check.

Here are some specific things you can say in a salary negotiation:

"I've done some research on the market value for this position and am seeing salaries a bit higher than what you've offered." This is a good way to start the negotiation by showing that you're aware of the market rate.

"I believe I bring excellent (list key skills) to the table." This is a good way to justify why you deserve a higher salary.

"I'm open to discussing the starting salary for this position." This shows that you're willing to negotiate and that you're not just accepting the first offer.

"I'm confident that I can make a significant contribution to your company." This is a good way to end the negotiation by showing that you're confident in your abilities.

Here are some benefits that you can negotiate:

Salary: This is the most obvious benefit to negotiate. However, it's important to remember that salary is not the only factor that determines your total compensation package.

Bonuses: Bonuses can be a great way to increase your earnings. However, it's important to understand how bonuses are calculated before you negotiate them.

Commissions: Commissions are a great way to earn money based on your performance. However, it's important to understand how commissions are structured before you negotiate them.

Benefits: Benefits can include things like health insurance, retirement savings plans, and paid time off. These benefits can be worth a lot of money, so it's important to negotiate them as well.

Negotiating salaries and benefits can be a challenge, but it's worth it if you want to get the best possible deal. By following these tips, you can increase your chances of success.

Chapter 4:

Diversifying Income Streams

Diversifying your income streams is a great way to protect yourself financially. If one source of income dries up, you'll still have others to rely on. There are many different ways to diversify your income, so you can find options that fit your skills, interests, and goals.

A few ideas for diversifying your income streams:

Start a side hustle. This could be anything from freelancing to selling handmade goods to starting a blog.

Invest in real estate. This could be rental properties, REITs, or even peer-to-peer lending.

Create passive income streams. This could involve things like affiliate marketing, selling digital products, or creating online courses.

Take on contract work. This is a great way to supplement your income and gain new skills.

Start a small business. This is a big undertaking, but it can be very rewarding.

Leap into the gig economy. There are many ways to make money on-demand, such as driving for Uber or Lyft, delivering food for DoorDash, or pet sitting for Rover.

Invest in yourself. This could involve taking courses, getting certified, or networking with other professionals.

The best way to diversify your income is to find a mix of sources that you're passionate about and that fit your lifestyle. With a little effort, you can create a financial safety net that will help you weather any storm.

Here are some additional tips for diversifying your income streams:

Start small. Don't try to do too much too soon. Start with one or two new income streams and gradually add more as you get more comfortable.

Be patient. It takes time to build new income streams. Don't get discouraged if you don't see results immediately.

Be persistent. Don't give up on your dreams. Keep working hard and eventually you'll reach your goals.

Diversifying your income streams is a great way to improve your financial security. By following these tips, you can create a more stable and resilient financial future.

Exploring Passive Income Opportunities

Passive income is income that you receive on a regular basis, without having to actively work for it. There are many different ways to generate passive income, and the best approach for you will depend on your skills, interests, and financial goals.

Here are some popular passive income ideas:

Investing in real estate. This is a classic way to generate passive income. You can buy rental properties, invest in real estate investment trusts (REITs), or flip houses.

Starting a blog or website. If you have a passion for writing or creating content, you can start a blog or website and monetize it through advertising, affiliate marketing, or selling digital products.

Creating an online course. If you have expertise in a particular subject, you can create an online course and sell it through a platform like Udemy or Teachable.

Writing and selling e-books. This is another great way to share your knowledge and expertise with others, and it can be a very passive income stream once your e-book is published.

Renting out a room or property. If you have a spare room in your home, you can rent it out to a tenant. You can also rent out a vacation property or parking space.

Investing in stocks or bonds. This is a more traditional way to generate passive income. When you invest in stocks or bonds, you earn dividends or interest payments.

Starting a dropshipping store. This is a low-cost way to start an online store. You don't need to carry any inventory, and you only pay for the products that you sell.

Selling digital products. This could include anything from eBooks to software to music. Once you create the product, you can sell it over and over again.

These are just a few of the many passive income opportunities available. The best way to find the right opportunity for you is to explore your interests and skills, and then do some research to see what's possible.

Guidelines for generating passive income:

Start small. Don't try to do too much too soon. Start with a small project that you can manage, and then scale up as you learn and grow.

Be patient. It takes time to build a passive income stream. Don't expect to get rich overnight.

Be consistent. The key to generating passive income is to be consistent with your efforts. Keep creating content, keep investing, and keep learning.

Passive income can be a great way to supplement your income or achieve financial freedom. With a little effort, you can create a stream of income that will help you reach your financial goals.

Investing Wisely for Long-Term Growth

Investing wisely for long-term growth is a key to financial security. By following some simple tips, you can increase your chances of success.

1. Set your goals. What do you want to achieve with your investments? Are you saving for retirement, a down payment on a house, or your child's education? Once you know your goals, you can start to develop a plan to reach them.

2. Understand your risk tolerance. How much risk are you comfortable taking with your investments? If you're not sure, start by taking a risk assessment quiz. This will help you determine the level of risk that's right for you.

3. Diversify your portfolio. Don't put all your eggs in one basket. Spread your money across different asset classes, such as stocks, bonds, and real estate. This will help to reduce your risk if one asset class performs poorly.

4. Invest for the long term. The stock market is volatile in the short term, but it has historically trended upwards over the long term. This means that if you stay invested for a long period of time, you're more likely to see your money grow.

5. Rebalance your portfolio regularly. As your investments grow, you'll need to rebalance your portfolio to ensure that it still meets your risk tolerance and goals. This means selling some of your winners and buying more of your losers.

6. Don't panic sell. When the market takes a downturn, it's tempting to sell your investments. However, this is usually the worst thing you can do. If you sell your investments when they're down, you'll lock in your losses. Instead, stay calm and ride out the storm.

7. Get help from a financial advisor. If you're not comfortable investing on your own, you can get help from a financial advisor. A financial advisor can help you develop a personalized investment plan and make sure that your investments are on track to meet your goals.

Investing wisely for long-term growth takes time, effort, and discipline. However, if you follow these tips, you'll be well on your way to financial security.

More tips for investing wisely for long-term growth:

Start investing early. The sooner you start investing, the more time your money has to grow.

Invest consistently. Even if you can only invest a small amount each month, it will add up over time.

Do your research. Before you invest in anything, make sure you understand the risks involved.

Don't be afraid to ask for help. If you're not sure where to start, talk to a financial advisor.

With careful planning and execution, you can achieve your long-term financial goals through investing.

Chapter 5:

Budgeting and Expense Management

Budgeting and expense management are two important financial concepts that can help you stay on track with your finances.

- Budgeting is the process of creating a plan for how you will spend your money. This includes tracking your income and expenses, and setting limits on how much you can spend in different categories.

- Expense management is the process of tracking and controlling your spending. This includes tracking your expenses, identifying areas where you can save money, and making adjustments to your budget as needed.

Budgeting and expense management can help you in a number of ways, including:

- Avoiding debt. By creating a budget and sticking to it, you can make sure that you are not spending more money than you have coming in. This can help you avoid debt, which can save you money in the long run.
- Reaching your financial goals. If you have specific financial goals, such as saving for a down payment on a house or retirement, budgeting can help you track your progress and make sure that you are on track to reach your goals.
- Peace of mind. Knowing where your money is going and being confident that you are not overspending can give you peace of mind. This can help you reduce stress and focus on other aspects of your

life.

If you are not sure where to start with budgeting and expense management, there are a number of resources available to help you. There are many budgeting apps and software programs that can help you track your income and expenses, and there are also many books and websites that offer tips on how to budget and manage your money.

Here are some tips for budgeting and expense management:

- Start by tracking your income and expenses. This will give you a good understanding of where your money is going.
- Set realistic goals. When you are creating your budget, make sure that your goals are realistic. If you set your goals too

high, you are more likely to give up.

- Be flexible. Your budget is not set in stone. As your income and expenses change, you will need to adjust your budget accordingly.
- Make it a habit. The best way to stick to your budget is to make it a habit. Track your spending regularly and review your budget monthly.

Budgeting and expense management can be a challenge, but it is worth it. By following these tips, you can learn how to manage your money effectively and reach your financial goals.

Creating a Practical Budget Plan

Here are the steps on how to create a practical budget plan:

Calculate your net income. This is the amount of money you have left after taxes and other deductions. You can find your net income on your pay stub or by using a budgeting tool.

Track your spending. This will help you see where your money is going each month. You can track your spending using a budgeting tool, a spreadsheet, or even just a notebook.

Set realistic goals. What do you want to achieve with your budget? Do you want to save for a down payment on a house? Pay off debt? Build up your emergency fund? Once you know your goals, you can start to create a budget that will help you reach them.

Make a plan. This is where you will assign your income to different categories, such as housing, transportation, food, entertainment, and savings. You can use the 50/30/20 rule as a starting point, or you can create a budget that works for your individual needs.

Adjust your spending to stay on budget. This is the most important step! It's important to review your budget regularly and make adjustments as needed. If you're overspending in one area, you may need to cut back in another.

Review your budget monthly. This will help you stay on track and make sure your budget is still working for you. If you need to make any changes, you can do so at this time.

Here are some additional tips for creating a practical budget plan:

Be as specific as possible when tracking your spending. This will help you see where your money is really going.

Don't be afraid to adjust your budget as needed. Your needs and priorities may change over time, so it's important to be flexible.

Make your budget a living document. This means that you should review it regularly and make changes as needed.

Don't get discouraged if you don't stick to your budget perfectly. Just keep trying and you'll eventually get there.

Creating a budget can be a challenge, but it's worth it in the long run. A budget can help you reach your financial goals, save money, and reduce stress. So what are you waiting for? Start creating your budget today!

Cutting Unnecessary Costs

Cutting unnecessary costs is a great way to save money and improve your financial situation.

Here are some tips on how to cut unnecessary costs:

Start tracking your spending. This is the first step to identifying where your money is going. You can use a budgeting app or simply track your spending in a spreadsheet.

Create a budget. Once you know where your money is going, you can create a budget to help you track your spending and stay on track. There are many different budgeting methods out there, so find one that works for you.

Cancel unnecessary subscriptions. Do you really need that streaming service you never use? Or that gym membership you only go to once a month? Take a look at your subscriptions and cancel the ones you don't use.

Reduce your energy consumption. There are many ways to reduce your energy consumption, such as turning off lights when you leave a room, unplugging appliances when they're not in use, and weatherizing your home.

Eat at home more often. Eating out can be expensive, so try to cook more meals at home. This is a great way to save money and eat healthier.

Shop around for better deals. Before you make a purchase, take some time to shop around and compare prices. You may be surprised at how much you can save by shopping around.

Use coupons and promo codes. There are many ways to find coupons and promo codes, such as online, in magazines, and in newspapers. Using coupons and promo codes can help you save money on your purchases.

Take advantage of free or low-cost activities. There are many free or low-cost activities available, such as going for a walk, visiting a museum, or attending a free concert. These are great ways to save money and have fun.

By following these tips, you can cut unnecessary costs and save money. This will help you reach your financial goals and improve your overall financial situation.

Here are some additional tips for cutting unnecessary costs:

Consider your lifestyle. What are your priorities? What are you willing to give up in order to save money?

Be realistic. Don't try to cut too much too soon. Start with small changes and gradually make more changes as you get used to them.

Be patient. It takes time to see the results of cutting unnecessary costs. Don't get discouraged if you don't see results immediately.

Cutting unnecessary costs can be a challenge, but it's worth it. By following these tips, you can save money and improve your financial situation.

Chapter 6:

Entrepreneurship and Business Ventures

Entrepreneurship is the process of starting and running a business venture. It is a risky but potentially rewarding endeavor. Entrepreneurs are individuals who are willing to take risks and who are passionate about their ideas. They are also typically good at problem-solving and at managing people and resources.

A business venture is a new business that is being started. It can be a small business or a large business. Business ventures can be started by entrepreneurs or by established businesses.

There are many different types of business ventures. Some common types of business ventures include:

- Retail businesses
- Service businesses
- Manufacturing businesses
- Technology businesses
- Food businesses
- Healthcare businesses
- Education businesses
- Financial services businesses

The success of a business venture depends on a number of factors, including the strength of the business idea, the quality of the management team, the availability of capital, and the overall business environment.

Here are some examples of entrepreneurial ventures:

- Apple was founded by Steve Jobs and

Steve Wozniak in 1976. The company started out as a computer repair shop, but it quickly grew into a major player in the personal computing industry.

- Amazon was founded by Jeff Bezos in 1994. The company started out as an online bookstore, but it has since expanded to sell a wide variety of products and services.
- Facebook was founded by Mark Zuckerberg, Eduardo Saverin, Dustin Moskovitz, and Chris Hughes in 2004. The company started out as a social networking website for Harvard University students, but it has since grown into the largest social media platform in the world.

These are just a few examples of the many successful entrepreneurial ventures that have been launched over the years. If you are thinking about starting your own business, there are a number of resources available to help you get started. You can find information on how to write a business plan, how to raise capital, and how to market your business. There are also a number of organizations that can provide you with support and advice.

If you are willing to take risks and are passionate about your ideas, then entrepreneurship could be a great career path for you. With hard work and dedication, you can achieve your goals and build a successful business venture.

Launching a Successful Startup

Launching a successful startup is no easy feat. It takes hard work, dedication, and a lot of luck. But if you're willing to put in the effort, it's definitely possible. Here are some tips to help you launch your startup successfully:

Do your research. Before you launch your startup, it's important to do your research and make sure there's a market for your product or service. You need to understand your target audience and what their needs are. You also need to research your competition and see what they're doing.

Create a business plan. A business plan is essential for any startup. It will help you define your goals, identify your target market, and develop a strategy for achieving success. Your business plan should be detailed and well-written.

Build a strong team. No one can launch a successful startup on their own. You need to build a team of talented and dedicated people who share your vision. Your team should have a mix of skills and experience.

Get funding. Unless you're lucky enough to have the financial resources to launch your startup on your own, you'll need to get funding. There are a number of ways to get funding, including angel investors, venture capitalists, and crowdfunding.

Market your product or service. Once you have your product or service ready to go, you need to start marketing it. This includes creating a website, developing a social media presence, and attending industry events.

Provide excellent customer service. Customer service is essential for any business, but it's especially important for startups. You need to make sure your customers are happy and satisfied with your product or service.

Be patient and persistent. Launching a successful startup takes time and effort. Don't get discouraged if you don't see results immediately. Just keep working hard and eventually you'll achieve your goals.

Here are some additional tips to help you launch your startup successfully:

Be flexible and adaptable. Things don't always go according to plan, so it's important to be flexible and adaptable. Be willing to change your plans if necessary.

Learn from your mistakes. Everyone makes mistakes, but it's important to learn from them. Don't dwell on your mistakes, but use them as an opportunity to improve.

Celebrate your successes. It's important to celebrate your successes, no matter how small they may seem. This will help you stay motivated and keep moving forward.

Launching a successful startup is a challenge, but it's also an incredibly rewarding experience.

If you're willing to put in the effort, it's definitely possible to achieve your goals.

Scaling and Sustaining Your Business

Scaling and sustaining your business is a complex process that requires careful planning and execution. Here are some tips to help you get started:

Define your goals. What do you want to achieve by scaling your business? Do you want to increase sales, market share, or profitability? Once you know your goals, you can start to develop a plan to achieve them.

Assess your current capabilities. What are your strengths and weaknesses? What resources do you have available? It's important to have a clear understanding of your current capabilities before you start scaling your business.

Invest in the right infrastructure. As your business grows, you'll need to invest in the right infrastructure to support it. This includes things like technology, people, and processes.

Create a scalable business model. Your business model should be designed to be scalable, so that you can easily grow without sacrificing efficiency or profitability.

Focus on customer satisfaction. Happy customers are more likely to stay with your business and help you grow. Make sure you're providing them with a great customer experience.

Build a strong team. A strong team is essential for scaling a business. Make sure you're hiring the right people and providing them with the training and support they need to succeed.

Be patient. Scaling a business takes time and effort. Don't expect to see results overnight. Be patient and persistent, and you'll eventually achieve your goals.

Here are some additional tips for sustainable scaling:

Focus on efficiency. As your business grows, it's important to find ways to become more efficient. This will help you reduce costs and improve profitability.

Invest in technology. Technology can help you automate tasks, improve communication, and streamline your operations. This can free up your time and resources so you can focus on growing your business.

Build relationships. Strong relationships with your customers, suppliers, and partners can help you grow your business sustainably. Make sure you're investing in these relationships and maintaining them over time.

Be adaptable. The business landscape is constantly changing, so it's important to be adaptable. Be prepared to change your business model, strategies, and tactics as needed to stay ahead of the competition.

Scaling and sustaining your business is a challenging but rewarding process. By following these tips, you can increase your chances of success.

Chapter 7:

Financial Planning for the Future

Financial planning for the future is important because it can help you:

- Set realistic goals and track your progress. A financial plan will help you define your financial goals and create a roadmap for achieving them. This can help you stay on track and make sure you're on the right track to reach your goals.
- Reduce your stress about money. When you have a financial plan, you have a better understanding of your finances and where your money is going. This can help you feel more in control of your finances and reduce your stress about money.

- Protect your assets. A financial plan can help you protect your assets from unexpected events, such as job loss, illness, or death. This can help you maintain your standard of living and ensure that your loved ones are taken care of.

- Plan for retirement. Retirement planning is one of the most important aspects of financial planning. A financial plan can help you determine how much money you need to save for retirement and how to invest your money to reach your goals.

Here are some steps you can take to start financial planning for the future:

1. Gather your financial information. This includes your income, expenses, assets, and liabilities.
2. Set your financial goals. What do you

want to achieve with your money? Do you want to buy a house, retire early, or send your kids to college?

3. Create a budget. A budget will help you track your income and expenses so you can see where your money is going.

4. Invest your money. Investing your money can help you grow your wealth over time.

5. Review your plan regularly. Your financial situation will change over time, so it's important to review your plan regularly to make sure it's still on track.

If you're not sure where to start, you can work with a financial advisor. A financial advisor can help you assess your financial situation, set goals, and create a plan to achieve your goals.

Additional tips for financial planning for the future:

Start early. The earlier you start saving and investing, the more time your money has to grow.

Live below your means. This will free up more money to save and invest.

Be consistent. Even if you can only save a small amount each month, it will add up over time.

Rebalance your portfolio regularly. This will help you stay on track with your risk tolerance and investment goals.

Review your plan regularly. Your financial situation will change over time, so it's important to review your plan regularly to make sure it's still on track.

Financial planning for the future is an important part of ensuring your financial security. By following these tips, you can set yourself up for a successful financial future.

Retirement Planning and Pension Options

Retirement planning is important for everyone, but it can be especially daunting if you don't know where to start. Here are some things to consider when planning for retirement:

Your current age and retirement goals. How much money do you need to save to live comfortably in retirement? When do you want to retire?

Your expected income in retirement. Will you have a pension? Social Security benefits? Other sources of income?

Your expenses in retirement. How much will you spend on housing, food, transportation, healthcare, and other essentials?

Your risk tolerance. How comfortable are you with taking on risk in your investments?

Your time horizon. How long do you have until you retire?

Once you've considered these factors, you can start to think about specific retirement plans and pension options. Here are a few of the most common:

Defined benefit pensions. These plans guarantee a certain income stream in retirement. They are typically offered by employers, but they are becoming less common. Defined contribution plans. These plans allow you to contribute a certain amount of money each year, and your employer may match some or all of your contributions. The money in these plans grows tax-deferred, and you can withdraw it in retirement.

Individual retirement accounts (IRAs). These plans are offered by financial institutions, and you can contribute up to a certain amount each year. The money in IRAs grows tax-deferred, and you can withdraw it in retirement.

Annuities. These are insurance products that provide a guaranteed income stream in retirement.

There are many other retirement plans and pension options available, so it's important to do your research and find the ones that are right for you. You should also work with a financial advisor to help you develop a comprehensive retirement plan.

Here are some additional tips for retirement planning:

Start saving early. The earlier you start saving, the more time your money has to grow.

Save as much as you can. The more you save, the more comfortable your retirement will be.

Invest wisely. Choose investments that are appropriate for your risk tolerance and time horizon.

Rebalance your portfolio regularly. This will help you keep your investments on track with your goals.

Get professional help. A financial advisor can help you develop a comprehensive retirement plan and make sure you're on track.

Retirement planning can be complex, but it's important to start planning early. By taking the time to understand your options and develop a plan, you can help ensure that you have a comfortable and secure retirement.

Tax Strategies for Optimizing Earnings

Here are some tax strategies for optimizing earnings:

Contribute to tax-advantaged accounts. This includes retirement accounts, such as 401(k)s and IRAs, as well as health savings accounts (HSAs). Contributions to these accounts are made with pretax dollars, which reduces your taxable income.

Donate to charity. You can deduct charitable contributions from your taxable income, up to certain limits. You can also donate appreciated assets, such as stocks, which can help you avoid capital gains taxes.

Take advantage of tax credits. There are a number of tax credits available, such as the child tax credit, the earned income tax credit, and the American Opportunity Tax Credit.

These credits can help you reduce your tax bill or even get a refund.

Defer taxes on capital gains. If you sell an investment that has appreciated in value, you will owe capital gains taxes on the profit. However, you can defer taxes on those gains by selling them in a tax-deferred account, such as a traditional IRA or a 401(k).

Invest in municipal bonds. Interest income from municipal bonds is typically exempt from federal income tax. This can be a good way to generate tax-free income, especially if you are in a high tax bracket.

Structure your income strategically. The way you earn your income can have a big impact on your tax bill. For example, business income is typically taxed at a lower rate than wage income. You may also be able to reduce your tax bill by shifting income from one year to another.

These are just a few of the many tax strategies that you can use to optimize your earnings. It is important to work with a tax advisor to develop a plan that is right for you.

Here are some additional tips for optimizing your earnings:

Keep good records. This will help you track your income and expenses, which is essential for tax planning.

Pay attention to the tax laws. The tax laws are constantly changing, so it is important to stay up-to-date on the latest changes.

Don't be afraid to ask for help. If you are not sure how to optimize your earnings, talk to a tax advisor. They can help you understand the tax laws and develop a plan that is right for you.

Chapter 8:

Overcoming Financial Challenges

Overcoming financial challenges can be difficult, but it is possible with hard work and dedication. Here are some tips to help you get started:

Identify the problem. What is the underlying cause of your financial challenges? Are you living beyond your means? Do you have too much debt? Once you know the problem, you can start to develop a plan to address it.

Create a budget. A budget is a great way to track your income and expenses so that you can see where your money is going. Once you have a budget, you can make adjustments to reduce your spending and free up more money to pay down debt or save for your future.

Pay down debt. If you have debt, it is important to focus on paying it down as quickly as possible. The longer you carry debt, the more interest you will pay. There are many different debt repayment strategies, so find one that works for you and stick to it.

Save for your future. It is important to have savings for unexpected expenses, such as car repairs or medical bills. You should also save for retirement so that you have a comfortable income when you are no longer working.

Get help if you need it. If you are struggling to overcome your financial challenges on your own, there are many resources available to help you. You can talk to a financial advisor, counselor, or credit counselor. They can help you develop a plan to get your finances on track.

Overcoming financial challenges takes time and effort, but it is possible. By following these tips, you can improve your financial situation and achieve your financial goals.

Here are some additional tips that can help you overcome financial challenges:

Get organized. This means having a system for tracking your income and expenses, as well as your debt and savings. There are many different tools and apps that can help you get organized, so find one that works for you.

Be patient. It takes time to overcome financial challenges. Don't get discouraged if you don't see results immediately. Just keep working at it, and you will eventually reach your goals.

Don't give up. There will be times when you feel like giving up. But it is important to remember that you can overcome your financial challenges if you don't give up. Just keep working hard, and you will eventually reach your goals.

I hope these tips help you overcome your financial challenges. Remember, you are not alone. There are many people who have faced financial challenges and overcome them. With hard work and dedication, you can too.

Dealing with Debt and Credit Management

Tips on how to deal with debt and credit management:

Make a budget. This is the first and most important step in managing your debt. Once you know where your money is going, you can start to make changes to free up more money to pay down your debt. There are many different budgeting tools and apps available to help you get started.

Contact your creditors. If you are struggling to make your payments, don't be afraid to contact your creditors. Many creditors are willing to work with you to create a payment plan that you can afford.

Consider debt consolidation. If you have multiple debts, consolidating them into one loan can make it easier to manage your payments. However, be sure to shop around and compare interest rates before you consolidate your debt.

Get help from a credit counselor. If you are feeling overwhelmed by your debt, a credit counselor can help you create a debt management plan. Credit counselors can also negotiate with your creditors on your behalf to get lower interest rates and monthly payments.

Be patient. It takes time to pay off debt. Don't get discouraged if you don't see results immediately. Just keep making progress and you will eventually reach your goal.

Here are some additional tips for managing debt and credit:

Pay more than the minimum payment. This will help you pay off your debt faster and save money on interest.

Avoid using credit cards for unnecessary purchases. Only use credit cards for things you can afford to pay off in full each month.

Review your credit reports regularly. Make sure there are no errors on your reports that could be affecting your credit score.

Ask for a credit limit increase. This can give you more breathing room if you need to make a large purchase or unexpected expense.

Managing debt can be challenging, but it is possible. By following these tips, you can get your debt under control and improve your financial future.

Handling Financial Emergencies

Financial emergencies can happen to anyone, at any time. A job loss, a medical emergency, or a natural disaster can all put a strain on your finances. If you're faced with a financial emergency, it's important to stay calm and take steps to get your finances back on track.

How to handle a financial emergency:

Assess your situation. What is the nature of the emergency? How much money will you need to cover the expenses? How long will the emergency last?

Prioritize your expenses. Make sure you're covering your essential expenses, such as housing, food, and healthcare. You can cut back on non-essential expenses, such as dining out or entertainment, to free up more money.

Use your emergency fund. If you have an emergency fund, this is the time to use it. An emergency fund is a pool of money that you set aside for unexpected expenses. It's a good idea to have enough money in your emergency fund to cover 3-6 months of living expenses.

Look for additional income. If you need more money to cover your expenses, you may be able to find a part-time job or do some freelance work. You can also ask your family and friends for help.

Contact your creditors. If you're unable to make your payments on time, contact your creditors and explain your situation. They may be willing to work with you to create a payment plan that you can afford.

Seek professional help. If you're feeling overwhelmed, you may want to speak to a financial advisor. They can help you create a plan to get your finances back on track.

Here are some additional tips for handling a financial emergency:

Stay calm. It's easy to panic when you're faced with a financial emergency, but it's important to stay calm and make rational decisions.

Be organized. Keep track of your expenses and income so you can see where your money is going. This will help you make informed decisions about how to allocate your resources.

Don't make any major decisions. Don't make any major financial decisions, such as taking out a loan or selling your home, until you've had a chance to assess your situation and develop a plan.

Seek help if you need it. If you're feeling overwhelmed, don't be afraid to seek help from a financial advisor or other professional.

Handling a financial emergency can be challenging, but it's important to remember that you're not alone. There are resources available to help you get through this difficult time. By following these tips, you can get your finances back on track and recover from the financial emergency.

Chapter 9:

Giving Back and Philanthropy

Giving back and philanthropy are both important concepts that involve helping others. However, there are some key differences between the two.

Charity is typically focused on providing immediate relief to people and is often driven by emotions. For example, donating to a food bank to help people who are struggling to afford food is an act of charity.

Philanthropy is focused on helping people and solving their problems over the long-term. It is often more strategic and involves ongoing partnerships with community and nonprofit leaders. For example, funding a research project to find a cure for a disease is an act of philanthropy.

Both charity and philanthropy are important ways to give back to our communities and make a difference in the world. However, philanthropy is often seen as a more sustainable and impactful way to help others.

Benefits of giving back and philanthropy:
It helps others. This is the most obvious benefit of giving back. When we help others, we make a difference in their lives and make the world a better place.

It makes us feel good. Helping others can give us a sense of satisfaction and purpose. It can also make us feel more connected to our community and to humanity as a whole.

It can improve our health. Studies have shown that people who volunteer or donate to charity tend to be healthier, both physically and mentally.

It can help us learn and grow. When we get involved in philanthropic activities, we learn about different cultures and perspectives. We also learn about ourselves and what we are capable of.

If you are interested in giving back or philanthropy, there are many ways to get involved. You can donate money, volunteer your time, or start your own philanthropic organization. There are also many online resources that can help you find organizations that are working on causes that you care about.

No matter how you choose to give back, your efforts will make a difference. So please, get involved and start making a difference today!

The Joy of Charitable Contributions

There are many reasons why people choose to

give to charity. Some do it out of a sense of duty, while others do it to help those in need. But did you know that there are also physical, emotional, and spiritual benefits to charitable giving?

Physical benefits

- Studies have shown that giving to charity can lower blood pressure, reduce stress, and boost the immune system.
- Giving can also help to improve sleep quality and overall mood.
- In one study, people who gave to charity reported feeling happier and more fulfilled than those who didn't.

Emotional benefits

- Charitable giving can help to connect us with our community and make us feel like we're making a difference in the world.

- It can also help to boost our self-esteem and give us a sense of purpose.
- In one study, people who volunteered for a charity reported feeling more connected to others and more satisfied with their lives.

Spiritual benefits

- Many people find that charitable giving is a way to connect with their spiritual beliefs.
- It can help us to feel closer to God or a higher power.
- In one study, people who gave to charity reported feeling more connected to their faith and more at peace with themselves.

The joy of giving

The benefits of charitable giving are not just physical, emotional, and spiritual. There is also a real sense of joy that comes from giving to others.

- When we give to charity, we are helping to make the world a better place.
- We are also helping to connect with our community and make a difference in the lives of others.
- And, we are also giving ourselves a gift. The act of giving can make us feel happier, more fulfilled, and more connected to our community.

So, if you're looking for a way to improve your health, happiness, and sense of purpose, consider giving to charity. It's a gift that you'll never regret.

Here are some quotes about the joy of

charitable giving:

- "The joy of giving is greater than the receiving." - Maya Angelou
- "The more you give, the more you get." - Zig Ziglar
- "No act of kindness, no matter how small, is ever wasted." - Aesop
- "Think of giving not as a duty, but as a privilege." - Winston Churchill

So, what are you waiting for? Start giving today!

Making a Positive Impact on Society

Making a positive impact on society is something that we all can do, no matter how big or small. There are many ways to make a difference, and the best way to start is to find something that you are passionate about.

Some ideas for making a positive impact on society:

Volunteer your time to a cause you care about. There are many organizations that need volunteers, and your time can make a real difference in the lives of others.

Donate to a charity or nonprofit. Your donation can help to support important work that is making a difference in the world.

Get involved in your community. There are many ways to get involved in your community, such as volunteering, attending community events, or running for office.

Be kind to others. Small acts of kindness can make a big difference in someone's day.

Speak up for what you believe in. If you see something that is wrong, don't be afraid to speak up. Your voice can make a difference.

Educate yourself and others about important issues. The more you know, the more you can do to make a difference.

Be a role model for others. Your actions can inspire others to make a positive impact on society.

Making a positive impact on society is not always easy, but it is definitely worth it. When we all work together, we can make the world a better place.

Additional benefits of making a positive impact on society:

It can give you a sense of purpose and satisfaction.

It can help you to connect with others and build relationships.

It can make you feel good about yourself and your contributions to the world.

It can help to make the world a better place for everyone.

If you are looking for ways to make a positive impact on society, I encourage you to start by finding something that you are passionate about. There are many ways to make a difference, and even small acts of kindness can make a big impact. So get out there and start making a difference!

Chapter 10:

Achieving Financial Freedom

Financial freedom is the ability to live your life without having to worry about money. It means having enough money to cover your basic needs, as well as your wants and desires. It also means having the freedom to choose your work, your lifestyle, and your location.

There are many different paths to financial freedom, but there are some common steps that most people take. These steps include:

Set financial goals. What do you want to achieve with your money? Do you want to retire early? Buy a house? Travel the world? Once you know what you want, you can start to create a plan to get there.

Create a budget. This will help you track your income and expenses so that you can see where your money is going. Once you know where your money is going, you can start to make changes to save more and spend less.

Pay off debt. Debt can be a major obstacle to financial freedom. The sooner you can pay off your debt, the sooner you can start saving and investing for your future.

Start saving and investing. This is how you will build wealth over time. There are many different ways to save and invest, so you can find an approach that works for you.

Live below your means. This means spending less money than you earn. It's not always easy, but it's one of the most important things you can do to achieve financial freedom.

Be patient and consistent. Achieving financial freedom takes time and effort. There will be setbacks along the way, but if you stay patient and consistent, you will eventually reach your goals.

Achieving financial freedom is not easy, but it is possible. By following these steps, you can start to build a better financial future for yourself.

Additional tips for achieving financial freedom:

Get educated about personal finance. There are many resources available to help you learn about personal finance. Books, websites, and financial advisors can all help you gain the knowledge you need to make sound financial decisions.

Get help from a financial advisor. If you're not sure where to start, a financial advisor can help you create a financial plan and make sure you're on track to achieve your goals.

Don't give up. There will be times when you feel discouraged or like you're not making any progress. But it's important to keep going. If you stay patient and consistent, you will eventually reach your goals.

Achieving financial freedom is a journey, not a destination. It's about making choices that will improve your financial situation over time. By following these tips, you can start to build a better financial future for yourself and your loved ones.

Steps to Financial Independence

Here are some steps you can take to achieve financial independence:

Set financial goals. What do you want to achieve financially? Do you want to retire early? Buy a house? Pay for your children's education? Once you know your goals, you can start making a plan to reach them.

Create a budget. This will help you track your income and expenses so you can see where your money is going. Once you know where your money is going, you can start making changes to save more.

Pay off debt. Debt can be a major obstacle to financial independence. If you have debt, focus on paying it off as quickly as possible.

Start saving. Once you've paid off your debt, start saving for your financial goals. This could include an emergency fund, retirement savings, or a down payment on a house.

Invest your money. Investing your money is a great way to grow your wealth over time. There are many different investment options available, so you can choose the ones that are right for you.

Live below your means. This means spending less money than you earn. This can be challenging, but it's essential if you want to reach financial independence.

Get educated about finances. The more you know about finances, the better equipped you'll be to make sound financial decisions. There are many resources available to help you learn about finances, such as books, websites, and financial advisors.

Here are some additional tips to help you reach financial independence:

Automate your savings. This will help you save money without even thinking about it.

Set financial milestones. This will help you stay motivated and on track.

Don't be afraid to ask for help. If you're struggling to reach financial independence, there are people who can help you, such as financial advisors or credit counselors.

Reaching financial independence takes time and effort, but it's definitely possible. By following these steps, you can be well on your way to achieving your financial goals.

What is the fastest way to reach financial independence?

There is no one-size-fits-all answer to this question, as the fastest way to reach financial independence will vary depending on your individual circumstances. However, some general tips that may help you reach financial independence faster include:

Earn more money. This may seem obvious, but the more money you earn, the more you can save and invest.

Live below your means. This means spending less money than you earn. This can be challenging, but it's essential if you want to reach financial independence faster.

Invest your money wisely. There are many different investment options available, so you can choose the ones that are right for you. However, it's important to do your research and invest wisely in order to maximize your returns.

Get help from a financial advisor. If you're struggling to reach financial independence on your own, a financial advisor can help you create a plan and track your progress.

It's important to remember that there is no magic bullet to financial independence. It takes time, effort, and dedication. However, if you follow these tips, you can reach your financial goals faster.

Maintaining Sustainable Wealth

Sustainable wealth is the ability to maintain a high standard of living over the long term, even in the face of economic downturns or other challenges. It is not just about having a lot of money, but also about having a sound financial plan and making wise investment decisions.

Tips for maintaining sustainable wealth:

Make a budget and stick to it. This is the foundation of any sound financial plan. By tracking your income and expenses, you can see where your money is going and make adjustments as needed.

Pay off debt as quickly as possible. Debt is a major drain on your wealth, so it's important to get rid of it as soon as you can. Start by paying off your high-interest debt first, then work your way down to your lower-interest debt.

Save for retirement. This is one of the most important things you can do to ensure your financial security in the future. Start saving early and contribute as much as you can afford.

Invest wisely. There are many different investment options available, so it's important to choose the ones that are right for you. Do your research and talk to a financial advisor to get started.

Protect your assets. This includes having adequate insurance coverage and estate planning. By taking steps to protect your assets, you can ensure that your wealth will be there for you when you need it.

Maintaining sustainable wealth takes time, effort, and discipline. But by following these tips, you can set yourself up for financial success in the long run.

Additional tips for maintaining sustainable wealth:

Be mindful of your spending. It's easy to overspend, especially if you're not tracking your spending. Make a habit of reviewing your budget and making adjustments as needed.

Set financial goals. Having specific goals will help you stay motivated and on track. Your goals could include saving for a down payment on a house, paying off debt, or retiring early.

Be patient. It takes time to build wealth. Don't get discouraged if you don't see results overnight. Just keep working at it and you will eventually reach your goals.

Remember, maintaining sustainable wealth is a marathon, not a sprint. By following these tips, you can set yourself up for financial success for many years to come.

Conclusion:

Recap of Key Learning

Identify your income streams. What are all the ways you earn money? This could include your salary, side hustles, investments, etc. Once you know where your money is coming from, you can start to think about how to increase it.

Set financial goals. What do you want to achieve with your money? Do you want to save for a down payment on a house, pay off debt, or retire early? Having specific goals will help you stay motivated and focused on increasing your earnings.

Invest in yourself. The best way to increase your earning potential is to invest in yourself. This could mean taking courses, attending workshops, or networking with people in your field. The more knowledge and skills you have, the more valuable you will be to employers or clients.

Be creative. There are many different ways to make money. Don't be afraid to think outside the box and come up with new ideas. The more creative you are, the more likely you are to find ways to increase your earnings.

Be persistent. It takes time and effort to increase your earnings. Don't give up if you don't see results immediately. Keep working hard and eventually you will reach your goals.

Here are some additional tips for mastering your earnings:

Track your spending. This will help you identify areas where you can cut back and free up more money to save or invest.

Live below your means. This means spending less money than you earn. This will give you a cushion in case of unexpected expenses and help you reach your financial goals faster.

Be patient. It takes time to build wealth. Don't expect to become a millionaire overnight. Just keep working hard and saving money, and eventually you will reach your goals.

I hope these tips help you master your earnings!

Embracing a Prosperous Future

The future is full of possibilities, and it is up to us to embrace them and create a prosperous future for ourselves and for generations to come. Here are some tips on how to embrace a prosperous future:

Be open to change. The world is constantly changing, and if we want to thrive in the future, we need to be open to change and willing to adapt. This means being willing to learn new things, try new things, and let go of old ways of doing things.

Be optimistic. A positive attitude is essential for creating a prosperous future. When we are optimistic, we are more likely to take risks, persevere in the face of challenges, and see opportunities where others see obstacles.

Be persistent. Nothing worth having comes easy. If we want to achieve our goals, we need to be persistent and never give up. This means staying focused on our goals, even when things get tough, and never giving up on our dreams.

Be creative. The future belongs to those who are creative and innovative. We need to be willing to think outside the box and come up with new ideas. This is how we will solve the problems of the future and create a better world for ourselves and for generations to come.

Be collaborative. We cannot achieve our goals alone. We need to work together with others to create a prosperous future. This means building relationships, collaborating with others, and sharing our ideas.

Embracing a prosperous future is not easy, but it is possible. By following these tips, we can create a better future for ourselves and for generations to come.

Here are some additional tips for embracing a prosperous future:

Educate yourself. The more you know, the better equipped you will be to succeed in the future.

Network with others. Get to know people who are working in your field or who have interests similar to yours.

Take risks. Don't be afraid to try new things and step outside of your comfort zone.

Be patient. It takes time to achieve success. Don't give up on your dreams.

The future is ours to create. Let's embrace it and make it a prosperous one for all.

Final Thoughts:

Congratulations on completing "Mastering Your Earnings"! Throughout this journey, we explored essential strategies and principles to help you take control of your finances and pave the way for a brighter financial future.

In this book, we delved into the significance of setting clear financial goals, creating a budget, and developing a sound investment plan tailored to your needs. By understanding the power of compounding, diversification, and risk management, you have gained the knowledge to navigate the complex world of finance with confidence.

Remember, mastering your earnings goes beyond accumulating wealth; it's about achieving financial freedom and security. Embrace the mindset of continuous learning and discipline as you implement the concepts learned here into your daily life.

As you move forward, always stay aware of your financial decisions, and never hesitate to seek advice from trusted experts. Surround yourself with like-minded individuals who support your financial goals, and remember that patience and perseverance are keys to long-term success.

This book is just the beginning of your financial journey. Your commitment to apply these principles will shape a prosperous future, not only for yourself but for generations to come. Empower yourself to be financially responsible, and let your newfound knowledge guide you towards the life you envision.

Thank you for joining us on this transformative experience. May you confidently embrace your financial journey, armed with the tools to master your earnings and live the life you deserve.

Here's to a life of financial abundance and fulfillment!

With best wishes,
Frank A. Hyman

www.ingramcontent.com/pod-product-compliance
Lightning Source LLC
Chambersburg PA
CBHW062326290526
45794CB00005B/1923